PIONEER SHOW FOLK

By Edith McCall

Exciting, amusing, true stories of pioneer show folk, stories of the real people who helped to develop the truly American Showboat, Minstrel Show and Wild West Show.

The Drake Players are the first to travel by wagon across the wilderness to Pittsburgh. They go on down the Ohio River by barge, bringing their plays to the pioneer settlements.

Rivers were the highways of the midwest. When the Chapmans drift downstream on a boat on which the shows can be given, the showboat is born.

Tom Rice borrows songs and rhythms and fun from Negroes on the riverside which become a part of the first Minstrel Show.

There is the story of Ralph Keeler, Minstrel Boy, who ends up on Doc Spaulding's *Floating Palace*.

Little Annie Moses, quail-shooter of Ohio, travels far as Annie Oakley with Buffalo Bill's *Wild West Show*.

Frontiers of America

PIONEER SHOW FOLK

By Edith McCall
Pictures by Carol Rogers

 CHILDRENS PRESS, CHICAGO

The *Frontiers of America* books are true stories of real people, told in simple, uncluttered text without losing the dramatic impact of the action and events. These books make stories of our country available to younger readers without sacrificing the vitality which makes them interesting to a wide age range.

Library of Congress Catalog Card Number: 63-15636

4 5 6 7 8 9 10 11 12 13 14 15 16 17 18 19 20 21 22 23 24 25 R 75 74 73 72 71 70 69

CONTENTS

The Drake Players Go West

Long ago, in the days when the whistle of the steamboat was a new sound and the puff and chug of a steam locomotive had not yet been heard in America, two creaky old covered wagons lumbered up a dusty road. They carried a company of actors and actresses to the Kentucky frontier, where they hoped to open the first theaters to bring shows to the pioneers.

"Whoa!" called out the driver of the first wagon. They had come into a little town. The horses stumbled to a stop in the shade of a tree on the roadside. It was a hot day in July and they had walked all day on that road in southern New York state, heading westward on the long journey from Albany to the Allegheny River.

"This as far as we go today, Mr. Drake?" called the driver of the second wagon. He had pulled his team in behind the lead wagon.

Mr. Drake leaned from the driver's seat to look back.

"Yes, Lewis. We'll post the bills for the show before we put up at the inn. Come on, boys!" He shouted to a group of four young men who were walking up the road. *"Forty Thieves* tonight!"

Mr. Lewis climbed down from the wagon seat, brushed the dust from his beaver hat, his "mutton chop" whiskers, the shoulders of his tail coat, and the knees of his striped trousers. Then, he turned back to the wagon. On the seat, a large, plump lady waited quietly.

"Come, my dear," said Mr. Lewis. "I will help you down. You and the young ladies will have time to rest in the shade of the tree."

The three young ladies of whom he spoke were climbing down from the rear of the lead wagon. They were Martha Drake, her young sister, Julia, and another actress named Fanny Denny. They were being helped down by Joe Tracy, who was the only one in the party who was not an actor. Joe kept the wagons in repair, tended the horses, helped put up scenery, shared the driving, and made himself useful in many other ways.

From one of the wagons, Mr. Drake pulled poster boards advertising the play, *Ali Baba and the Forty Thieves,* from the *Abrabian Nights.* As the young men reached him, he handed a bugle to one of them.

8

"Here, Noah. Give a few toots on the horn so the folks will come out to see what the hullabaloo is about."

To Noah Ludlow, even tooting the horn was exciting, like everything else in show business. The other three young men were sons of "Old Sam" Drake. Young Sam, Aleck and James had grown up as members of the "Drake Players," and had been acting in plays ever since they were old enough to walk onto a stage. But to Noah, it was all new. He was nineteen years old, and had left his home the year before to learn to act in Albany. This was his first time on the road with the Drake Players.

Old Sam hurried ahead to the courthouse that stood in the center of the little business square. He wanted to use the courtroom as a theater that evening, for there was no other room large enough in the town. In larger towns, the inn sometimes had a ballroom that made a better theater, but there would be no place that large until they finally reached Pittsburgh.

The young men knew what to do. Noah tooted the horn. Young Sam and James took hammer and nails and put up some posters on the trees. Over his shoulders, Aleck hung the "sandwich" boards with the pictures of Ali Baba poking his head out of the great

oil jar as the forty thieves, fierce of face but bright in red and yellow clothes, raised daggers over his head.

Old Sam waved from the courthouse door that all was set. Noah tooted loudly to draw a crowd. Aleck marched back and forth. Then Old Sam shouted.

"Come one, come all, to the courthouse tonight, folks! See before your very eyes the wonders of the Arabian Nights of old! See Ali Baba outwit forty thieves! The greatest company of actors ever to come to your city will present the finest, the *very* finest show you have ever seen! See the great chests of genuine jewels, the silks and satins of the Orient — all before your very eyes! Tonight, one night only! Do not miss the greatest show of your lifetime, here at seven o'clock, tonight! Here in the courthouse, folks!"

The next two hours were busy ones. The men brought rolled up scenery, boxes of needed things for the play, the curtain and candle footlights. A plain little court-room became a bit of far off Arabia.

Mr. Lewis had found sleeping rooms for the company at the inn. There Mrs. Lewis and the girls freshened up the costumes the best they could. In those days, it was hard to find bright colored cloth that would wash, and the costumes looked dingy in the

11

daylight. But at night, in the glow of the candle foot-lights, the dull, tarnished braid would become shining gold, the glass beads would be bright jewels, and the soiled costumes would become princely garments.

At seven, Noah peeked out through the closed curtains. The little courthouse was packed. The benches were filled to the last inch and there was standing room only for the latecomers. He remembered his first night as an actor. It had been in this same play, but he had been given only two words to say. Tonight he played the part of several of the thieves, popping in and out of sight often, each time with a different colored cap on his head to make it seem as if the four "thieves" in the company were really forty.

The clapping was loud and long when the play ended. This little town had been on the frontier only a few years ago, for this was the year 1815, and all the towns west of the Alleghenies were young. To many in the audience, this was the only play they would see all year. To the colonies along the seacoast, actors had come from Europe to bring to the people in America a little amusement besides the games and singing and dancing they had for fun. The cities of the east now had a few museums, a small circus now and then, and theaters to go to most of the year. But on the frontier, such things had not yet come.

The next morning, the two wagons were on their way again.

"From here on, we'll be in the wilderness, almost until we get to Pittsburgh, folks," Old Sam said. "No more places to give a play for a while, so we'll travel all day."

The woods closed in around them. Noah expected to see an Indian lurking behind a tree any moment. When he and the other boys had to go ahead to clear brush out of the overgrown trail so that the wagons could pass, he learned that he wasn't the only one who felt a little afraid. None of them had been much farther west than Philadelphia before. They all jumped at the sounds of little animals scurrying for cover.

At noon, Noah and Aleck were sent for dry firewood while the company camped at the side of a stream. They found a fallen tree, and were soon chopping off dead limbs. As he stood up with an armload of wood, Noah caught sight of a painted face looking at him over the bushes. He almost dropped the wood.

"Don't look now, Aleck, but we have a visitor," he said. He pretended he hadn't seen the red-brown face and the brush of black hair down the middle of the shaved head.

Aleck looked up questioningly. He was a little deaf. "What did you say, Noah?"

Noah quickly glanced back at the bushes. There was no face there now.

"Nothing, Aleck," he said. If he ever had to warn Aleck of Indians, he would have to shout so loudly that the whole tribe would know they had been seen.

He told Old Sam of what he had seen, off to one side where the ladies could not hear him. Old Sam nodded. "Yes, they told me back in town that we would soon see Indians. But don't worry, Noah. They are friendly. The ones that aren't friendly are farther west."

Noah didn't think that helped much. "Isn't that just where we are going?" he asked.

Mr. Drake said, "We'll stay south and east of the treaty lines, Noah. Don't you fear. It's forty years since Daniel Boone first went into Kentucky to live. A lot of people have moved into the western lands since then, or we wouldn't be planning to open theaters there. It isn't as wild as you think."

Noah thought the dark woods along the trail were

still about as wild as they could be. So were the animals that howled at night. But he learned there were more people in those woods than he thought. One afternoon, Mrs. Lewis was lost while she walked behind the wagons to get some exercise. The actors had just begun to search for her when two pioneers came and offered to help. Within an hour, there were eight more helping with the search. And four of them were Indians.

"You were right about the Indians being friendly, Mr. Drake," Noah said. "They must be friendly to spend hours looking for a woman they never saw."

They were all beginning to feel like frontiersmen themselves by the time their wagon journey ended. They had reached the wild Allegheny River at the little settlement of Olean. There they were to trade the wagons and horses for a boat. The fact that none of them had ever been on a flatboat before did not worry them.

"You just let it float down the river. There's no place to go except between the river banks," said Old Sam.

Noah looked at the boat that was to be their home for a month or two. There wasn't much to it. It was about 25 feet long and 15 feet wide, with board sides that rose five or six feet along most of its length. The sides were the walls of a roofed over cabin. The roof curved a little so that water would run off it.

In the cabin, there was room to stow the stage properties and costumes and the few other things the company had, but there was room to curtain off only two bedrooms. Mr. and Mrs. Lewis would have one, and the young ladies the other. The Drakes, Tracy and Noah would sleep wherever they could.

"What do they call a crate like this?" Noah asked Old Sam.

"It's a flatboat, boy, but the men here tell me this kind is called an ark."

Noah laughed. "Noah's Ark," he said. He kept that idea in mind. A year or two later, when he had his own company they traveled in *Noah's Ark*.

On the roof, at the middle of the stern, was a forked piece of wood in which rested the long handle of the steering oar. It was just a long pole with a wide board at the end that went into the water. There were a couple of loose poles on the boat, too, and a pair of oars for the little skiff, or rowboat, that was tied to the larger boat.

"Yo, ho, ho! It's off to sea we go," sang Young Sam. He and the other young men pushed the ark out into the Allegheny River, while Old Sam struggled with the heavy steering oar.

Just then, a young man in the uniform of a soldier of the War of 1812 came running down to the riverbank.

"Hey, there!" he yelled. "Could you use a good hand aboard?"

Old Sam was making strange splashings with the steering oar.

"Reckon we could," he said. "If we can stop this dang thing."

The young men leaned on the poles. They had not gone far enough for the current to take hold of the boat, but even so they had some trouble getting it close enough to shore for the young man to leap aboard.

"My name is Hull," he said. "I'm on my way home to Ohio after fighting in the war."

"Been on a riverboat much?" Old Sam asked.

"Not on the Allegheny, but twice up and down the Ohio, and down the Mississippi, too," said Hull. "Before I went into the army, I did a spell of keelboating."

"Good. We're actors, and not boatmen," said Old Sam. "I'll be obliged to have you take this confounded steering oar."

Hull took over, and soon the ark was following the

channel of the river. The other young men saw Hull take off his jacket and shirt, and did the same themselves, for the July afternoon sun was very hot. Hull was brown to the waist, and his muscles rippled. The other boys looked white and thin beside him.

The sun dropped behind the tree-lined shore and the river water blackened in shadow. Old Sam said, "Head for shore, Hull. We'll tie up for the night and do our cooking out in the open this warm evening."

Just ahead, a wooded island divided the river into two streams.

Hull said, "If you'll take a word of advice, Sir, you will camp on that island instead of on the mainland. Less chance of wild animals creeping up on you."

"Thank you, Hull. We'll do that," said Old Sam.

Soon the boat was tied to a sycamore tree that overhung the bank. After their days of traveling through the woods, the women knew just how to go about getting a meal in the wilderness. They made stew of some meat they had bought in Olean.

After supper, Martha and Julie Drake and Fanny Denny sang, while the men smoked their pipes or just lay back and looked up at the stars. After a half hour, the Lewises said good night and went to the boat to sleep.

"Come on, girls," said Martha. "We had better turn in, too."

Old Sam and Joe Tracy put blankets on the ground.

"I'm not sleepy yet," said Young Sam. "Why don't we take the skiff and go see what's on the mainland? Maybe there's a town just beyond the trees. I thought I saw lights a while ago."

The three Drake boys, Noah and Hull climbed into the skiff. James and Noah decided they would rather sit in the boat than go exploring. The others jumped ashore and soon disappeared into the woods. Noah and James stretched out in the little boat. The frogs croaked and the katydids argued, "Katy did — Katy didn't." The sounds made Noah and James sleepy. But they sat up, wide awake, at the sound of crashing dead tree limbs.

Noah said, "They are the noisiest pioneers that ever tracked through a woods."

Young Sam appeared and leaped into the boat. Aleck was right behind him. Hull came last. As he leaped into the boat, he grabbed the oar and gave the boat a good shove out into the stream.

When the skiff was about twenty feet from shore, Young Sam said, "No more exploring in the dark for me! We walked right up to two or three wolves. You should have heard them snarl!"

The wolves were howling noisily at the water's edge by then. The boys, back on the island, listened until at last the animals moved on.

"Maybe there are wolves on this island, too," said Aleck.

Hull said, "Likely there are. But if we keep the fire burning, they'll stay back."

They built up the fire. Soon everyone was asleep except Noah. He found himself thinking of the fire burning low each time he was about to drop off to sleep. By the time he put more wood on it, he was wide awake once more. At last he had an idea of how he could get some sleep.

He poked Aleck Drake. "Aleck, Aleck, wake up!"

"Huh?" said Aleck.

"Didn't you hear that howl? It was very close," said Noah.

"Fire'll keep the animals back," muttered Aleck. "Go to sleep."

A moment later, Noah poked him again. "Aleck!

Didn't you hear that? Even you should have been able to hear it. I am sure some animal is creeping up on us."

Aleck was wide awake this time. He got up and put some wood on the fire. Noah rolled over and was soon sound asleep. Aleck, straining his ears to hear sounds he was sure must be there, could not get back to sleep. He spent the rest of the night keeping the fire built up.

In the morning, they shoved off from the island and floated on down the river. It was a very hot day, too hot to lie in the sun on the roof, and too stuffy under the roof. They made an awning for themselves of some stage scenery. The breeze swept under it, and everyone on board stretched out in its shade. Even Hull, handling the steering oar, managed to lie down. He held the pole steady with his crossed legs.

The boat floated gently down the stream. Noah and Aleck were first to fall asleep after their wakeful night. The sound of their even breathing was too much for the others, and before long everyone was asleep. Even Hull dozed off.

Suddenly Mrs. Lewis screamed, "Look out, look out!"

Noah, without checking, jumped into the water, sure that one of the girls had rolled off the curved roof into the river. Someone was in the water, but it was

21

not one of the girls. Mr. Lewis, startled by his wife's scream, had rolled into the river and was splashing about.

"A waterfall! A waterfall!" screamed Mrs. Lewis, pointing down the river. "We'll go over it in a minute."

Hull was on his feet. Ahead, he saw that someone had built a mill dam right across the river. No boat could pass.

He shouted, "Every man who can swim jump overboard! Grab the boat and hold her with all you've got!"

Mr. Drake and Mr. Lewis leaned against the poles while all the young men jumped into the river. With all their strength, they pushed at the boat to stop its downstream drift. The dam made a little lake right there, and the current was not so strong as farther upriver. They managed to stop the boat just a few feet above the dam.

"Now, we've got to push or pull it upstream to safety," Hull said. "Can you hold it, boys, while I get a rope tied to her? We'll *cordelle* it back up the river."

The crew, with sleep well out of them, backwatered and pushed until they had the boat in shallow water at the stream's edge. Hull tied a heavy rope into a ring at the stern. While Tracy, Aleck and James held the boat in place, Young Sam, Noah and Hull got into the skiff and rowed upstream to where a tree overhung the bank. They took the coil of rope with them, letting it out as they moved away from the boat. When they reached the tree they wound it once around the trunk and beached the skiff.

"Pull!" called Hull. All three pulled with all their strength. Back on the boat, the other young men pushed. The boat began its upstream trip. When it was pulled up to the tree, the rope was taken upstream to another tree, and the job began again.

It was slow, hard work. All the men were wet with sweat as well as river water. The clumsy, square-ended, flat-bottomed ark was not built for upriver travel. At day's end, however, they were back at the point of the island where they had begun the day's journey.

"Why in Sam Hill would anyone be allowed to build a dam across a river which is supposed to be open to Pittsburgh?" Old Sam growled.

Hull went ashore to find out. When he came back, he had the answer.

"We took the wrong branch of the river," he said. "We should have gone down the other side of the island. There's a forking of the river here. That dam reached from a long, narrow island to the shore. We can get through by using the main channel."

There was no choice but to make camp on the island again. But this time, even Noah slept through the night.

"I've learned one thing," he said in the morning as he rubbed his aching muscles. "I am a better actor than a boatman."

As they moved the boat around to the main channel and began the day's journey, their young voices went up in song,

"Oh, fiddle dee, dee —
    It's an actor's life for me!"

The Drake Boat Show Moves On

The Drake Players, with Hull to guide the boat, had
a better day than the one before. They were stuck on
a sandbar for a few minutes, but jumping into the river
to lighten the load and to pull the boat free was only
play after the work of the day before. That night they
tied at the shore, near an old log barn. They went
inside, blocked the doorway, and slept through the
night. The boys had a safer feeling with some kind of
wall around them.

The next morning, Mrs. Lewis said, "The meat we
bought in Olean is about gone. Do you men think you
could get a farmer to sell us a pig, or maybe a lamb?"

"We will try, my dear," said Mr. Lewis. "Come,
Noah. You and I will go up to that farmhouse yonder,
and see if the farmer will sell us an animal to butcher."

"How will we get it back here?" Noah asked.

Mr. Lewis picked up the dagger that he used in one
of the plays. "I'm a pretty fair butcher," he said. "We'll
skin it and carry just the good meat back in the skin."

The two set off through the woods along the river

and were soon in a cleared field. Some sheep were grazing in the field.

"We'll get one of those, Noah," said Mr. Lewis. "We'll go up to the farmhouse and pay for one of them, and then come back here to butcher it."

A woman stood in the cabin doorway, watching them as they drew near.

"Good morning, madam," said Mr. Lewis. He spoke in his best stage voice, took off his hat and swept it low in a bow. "Is your husband at home?"

The woman was sure these men were up to no good. They were too polite for the frontier.

"What if he ain't?" she said. By this time, three children, all barefooted, were clinging to her skirt.

"Madam, it will please us to buy one of your sheep," Mr. Lewis said.

"They ain't for sale," said the woman. "Be off with you!"

Mr. Lewis begged, "Madam, we will pay you well, and we do need the meat badly, for a company of weary travelers on yon river."

"What be your business?" the woman asked.

Mr. Lewis bowed again. "We are members of the Drake Players, trained in the art of Shakespeare."

"Humph!" said the woman. "Play-actin' folks! I'll have no truck with such. Get out of here before I call my man. Git, now!"

She pushed the door shut in the men's faces, and slammed the wooden bar into place inside it.

"Come, Noah," said Mr. Lewis.

They walked back to the pasture.

"We must have one of those sheep," Mr. Lewis said. "We'll catch one for ourselves, Noah, and leave the money. Who's to stop us?"

Noah was not sure he liked the idea, but Mr. Lewis already had started after one of the sheep. The animals began to run, shy of the strangers. Noah circled around, trying to head off the one Mr. Lewis was chasing. It was running back towards the cabin clearing.

"Get it, Noah!" yelled Mr. Lewis.

Noah made a dive for the running sheep. He landed on its back, with his hands well into the wool on its shoulders.

"Whoa, there!" he yelled. He couldn't let go without danger of breaking his own bones, nor could he ride much farther in that strange position. Somehow, he pulled himself up until he was sitting on the sheep's back, still with his hands dug well into the wool.

There was a small log stable near the cabin. The sheep headed for it, running as it had never run before. On it went, with Noah holding on with all his might.

"Watch out, Noah!" yelled Mr. Lewis, who was running after Noah's strange mount.

Noah looked up. The sheep was heading into a low doorway in the stable, made as an entrance for animals and not for men. Noah saw that he would have to get off the sheep, and quickly. He let go and fell backward landing with a thud. He saw the blue sky above him for a moment, and then it was black as night.

He didn't know how much time had passed when he heard Mr. Lewis say, "Are you all right, Noah, my lad? We've got to get out of here. I've got the sheep all skinned."

Noah suddenly remembered where he was. He sat up carefully and felt the lump on the back of his head. He felt his arms and legs and tried standing up. He had no broken bones.

"I think I can walk," he said. "Come on. Let's get back to the ark."

"Not without the mutton," said Mr. Lewis. He had skinned and cleaned the sheep on which Noah had ridden to the stable.

There was no time for further work, for a man's voice was heard in answer to a call from the frontier woman. Mr. Lewis dropped three dollars in the sheep's wool. He took the front legs of the sheep and Noah the back, and away they ran. Noah staggered a little, but moving and the need for speed steadied him.

The woman was screaming, "Harry! Harry! Thieves!"

"Faster, boy," said Lewis. "Harry must be her husband."

Away they went, into the woods as they heard a man shout, "Stop, thieves!" A gun shot followed his cry.

The shore where the boat was tied was not far ahead. Lewis cried out, "Hull, get ready to shove off — fast!"

The two flung the sheep onto the ark and leaped on board as the Drake boys pushed on the poles. They were about thirty feet away when the angry sheep owner reached the shore. He aimed his shotgun at the boat and peppered the sides with buckshot.

Hull picked up his own rifle. He aimed at a slender tree branch that was right over the man's head. It bent instantly, pulling a leafy curtain over the angry farmer's face.

"Bravo!" shouted the Drake Players.

"He'll take a 'curtain call' any minute now," Old Sam said. "But we'll be out of reach of his shotgun by then. I hope he didn't put a hole in this old ark's sides."

The last the actors saw of the farmer, he was jumping up and down in a great rage. Mr. Lewis explained what had happened while Noah gently rubbed the bump on the back of his head.

"If *this* is an actor's life, I'm beginning to wonder if it really is 'An actor's life for me,' " Noah said.

But a day or two later, Noah felt a return of his love for acting. They reached a little town, and Old Sam decided they would stop long enough to give a show.

"We may soon need some more money to buy sheep," he said, winking at Mrs. Lewis. She had scolded her husband mightily for his way of buying meat.

The play Old Sam chose was a little comedy called, *No Song, No Supper.* In it, Mrs. Lewis was supposed to sing a song about a shepherd and his pet lamb.

The audience listened quietly as Mrs. Lewis sang, for her voice was sweet. At the end, Mr. Lewis, playing the part of the shepherd, had a line to say.

"Egad, Mabel! It was lucky you fell in with the sheep!"

The whole company of actors burst into laughter,

while the people of the audience looked at each other, wondering if they had missed a good joke. Never again could the Drake Players give that line without laughing.

Then the downriver journey went on. There were more settlements as they drew near to Pittsburgh at the end of the Allegheny River. There it met the Monongahela River from the south, and the two joined to form the beautiful Ohio. They would follow the Ohio to Louisville, Kentucky.

One night, the young actors frightened a group of mule sellers who smelled worse than their mules. The actors rented a room in an inn, but found the landlord had also rented it to the mule sellers.

"We'll have to get rid of them," said Young Sam. "I can't sleep with that smell in the room."

They had an idea, a plan which would make the mule sellers *want* to leave.

All of the boys knew the lines of Shakespeare's play, *Hamlet.* In the play, a ghost is seen moving about outdoors. One of the boys dressed in a sheet and walked back and forth outside the window of the inn. The other boys used the lines from the play to talk to each other as the mule sellers listened.

Noah said, "Has the thing appeared again tonight?"

Aleck peered out the window and said, "I have seen nothing."

Just then, the ghost appeared at the window. The mule sellers nudged each other and their mouths fell open.

The ghost disappeared, but a moment later it was back.

"On him, on him! Look you, how pale he glares!" cried Noah.

The mule sellers had seen enough. They ran from the room without stopping to dress. The actors burst out laughing as the ghost came inside. Then they picked up the smelly clothes and tossed them out the window. Soon they were all asleep.

When they reached Pittsburgh, the Drake Players found a hall in which to give their plays, and stopped for a few days to earn some money.

Then on they went, down the Ohio River, the first company of actors to travel to the frontier to bring pleasure into the lives of the people of the American wilderness.

Their idea of using a boat in order to reach the settlements was picked up by others soon afterward. This was a new thing for actors anywhere to do, something purely American. It was done because the American frontier had few roads, and because of the great river system of the central part of the United States. The Missouri-Mississippi-Ohio Rivers and their branches were the real highways for many years. The "boat show," as such traveling companies were called, was father of the great American "showboat."

Before long, Noah Ludlow had his own boat show company, traveling from landing to landing in his *Noah's Ark*. But, like other boat shows, they could give shows only where there was a room large enough, and many little frontier settlements had none.

About fifteen years after the Drake Players came down the river, another family of actors, the Chapman family had the idea of building a boat large enough so that shows could be given right on the boat. This was the "showboat," and its coming to a tiny frontier settlement was often the brightest day in a long year for many a hard-working pioneer.

The Chapman Showboat

Mama Chapman sat bent over her sewing in a room of the stuffy old inn at Pittsburgh. The Chapman Players' boat show had been stopped in that city for a long time, but soon they would be moving on.

Mama moved closer to the open casement windows to catch the late afternoon light and bent over the pieces of red cloth she was sewing onto a white background.

"To be, or not to be —" shouted her oldest son, William Chapman, Jr. Mama did not even look up from her work. She was quite used to hearing William shout lines from Shakespeare's plays. An actor had to practice.

"Be Horatio for me, Mama," he said.

Mama sewed on, giving "Horatio's" lines without looking up. All of the Chapman Company knew *Hamlet* well. They had played in England until 1827, just four years ago. Then they had come to America, soon leaving the big cities to become a "boat show."

Mr. Chapman had seen right away that it would save a lot of trouble to have a large enough boat so that the shows could be given on it. He was surprised that no one had tried it before.

William went on with his lines from *Hamlet*. "My father — methinks I see my father."

Mama "Horatio" said, "Oh where, my lord?"

Just then "Papa" Chapman came into the room. "Right here, coming in the door," he said. "And I've good news for you! Tomorrow we can launch the showboat. It is ready at last."

Mama dropped her sewing. William forgot his lines. The three danced around the room in joy. Another young man came in to learn the reason for the excitement.

"The boat is ready, George," said Mama. "Tomorrow it goes into the water. The next day we leave this town where people are so busy building boats they have no time for the theater."

"Caroline!" George called into the hallway. "Come here — good news!"

Caroline Chapman, thirteen years old but already a favorite and star in the Chapman Company, came in, followed by William's wife, Phoebe. A few minutes later, two children came in from playing on the street outside the hotel. One was ten-year-old Harry, whose father and mother were dead, and who lived with his Grandma and Grandpa Chapman. The little girl with him was really his aunt, though she was about his own age. She was Therese Sarah, youngest of the children of the Chapman family.

Harry loved to tease the girl. "Aunty, did you hear the news?" he asked. "Aunty" wrinkled her nose at him. "We'll be floating down the Ohio in a day or so."

Phoebe, who sang beautifully, started the song she had learned from the boatmen while she had watched the building of the new showboat down at the boat-yards. The others joined in with her on the chorus.

"The boatman is a lucky man,
No one can do as the boatman can,
The boatmen dance and the boatmen sing,
The boatman is up to everything.
 HI-O, away we go,
 Floating down the river of the O-Hi-o!"

They all linked hands and danced in a circle in the hotel room. But the dance didn't last long, for the landlord began to pound on the ceiling of the room below with a broom handle.

"Thank goodness, we'll soon be living on the boat and can dance and sing when we feel like it," said

Phoebe. "Anyway, it is time to eat supper and get into costume for tonight's show."

They gave their plays in the dining hall of the inn. The landlord was afraid his hotel would get a bad name if they gave any plays other than those by Shakespeare, so they were giving *Hamlet.*

Show folks were looked down on by the townspeople, anyway, and the landlord did not want anyone to think he was housing the kind who played in low comedies.

The next day, all the Chapmans went down to the boatworks. Mama Chapman had stayed up after the others went to bed, working on her sewing. She had finally finished it about two o'clock in the morning. Now she carried it, rolled up, as she went to see the new showboat.

Papa led the way down to the water's edge. There, gleaming white with fresh paint, was a different kind of boat from any ever seen before. Its lower part was a flat barge, about one-hundred-twenty feet long but quite narrow. In place of the low cargo box that was usually built onto such barges was a box-like building, which took up about one-hundred feet of the deck space. It had double doors at one end. Along its sides ran a row of square windows.

"Come aboard, everyone!" Papa called. He nelped Mama up the gangplank.

Mama unrolled her bundle of sewing. It was a big white banner, with red letters sewed onto it, FLOAT-ING THEATRE.

"First, let's put up the flag," Mama said. "I finished it just in time."

Papa lined them all up to watch the hanging of the flag. William climbed the ladder that led to the roof, took the flag to the stern of the boat where a pole had been fastened for it, and ran the cord through the eyelets Mama had embroidered into the flag's end. As if in salute, a breeze came up just in time, and set the banner to waving.

"Hurrah!" cried the Chapmans.

"Now let's see the theater," said Papa. Harry and Sarah ran ahead to open the double doors.

"Oh, it's beautiful!" Sarah said.

Soon all the family were in the theater room. It had a stage at the far end. Rows of backless benches were in place for the audience. Above the entrance doors, the ceiling was very low, for it formed the floor for a balcony where more people could be seated.

"The dressing rooms and our living quarters are

beyond the stage," said Papa. Soon they were all admiring the way everything they needed had been provided. There was a little kitchen with a cookstove such as the steamboats had in their galleys.

The next morning, the first showboat in the world began its trip down the Ohio River. The Chapmans had hired a boatman to steer the long flatboat, but the young Chapmans all helped shove off from shore.

"Now," said Papa, when they had all waved good-by to the boatbuilders at the dock, "we shall get ready to do our first play. No more Shakespeare for a while. We'll do *The Stranger* for this evening's show."

But rehearsals had to wait. The morning breeze had come up and the flag waved beautifully, but the boat seemed almost to be standing still. The breeze blew directly upriver, and the big theater building met it squarely. Harry, George, William and the extra actor Papa had hired for the trip all had to help pole the boat to keep it moving downstream.

The river was full of other boats, and Papa was glad they had a boatman to steer the showboat. The lower, smaller boats drifted past the big showboat. There were all kinds of them, but on each, the people turned to stare at the big showboat and to read the letters on its waving flag.

First came an open raft. On it, a ragged tent had been pitched. A hen and a rooster were trying to free themselves from the cords tied to one leg of each. A hog was also leg-tied to a pole driven between the floorboards of the raft. A woman in a ragged, dirty dress sat on the family's only chair, for all the world like a queen enthroned among her subjects. A little pile of dishes and a couple of pots and pans and a battered old round-top trunk were beside her. A baby crawled near the edge of the raft, but no one seemed to mind. Six ragged boys poled the raft, while their lean, bearded father steered. Along with many other families, they were "going west," bound for a clearing on the frontier in Illinois, Missouri or Arkansas.

As the raft came alongside the showboat, the boys stopped poling to stare.

"Now what in tarnation?" the man asked.

"Don't know, Paw," said the oldest boy. "Hey, Lem — ye've been to school. What do that air writing on that flag say?"

"Floating t-h-e-a-t-r-e," he spelled out. "Don't know what that word is."

41

George Chapman, poling hard, heard their talk. "It's a floating theater, sonny. Look for us tonight when you tie up. We'll be giving the first show on board the Chapman Floating Theater."

Mouths fell open, as the boys stared. "Git to that polin' boys. We ain't got all day to be gapin' at no lowdown showfolks," said their Pa.

The raft moved on, but along came an ark, much like that of the Drake Players. On the open end of its deck were farm animals. There was a team of horses, two milking cows, a pair of hogs, and a coop full of chickens. The Chapmans could see the parts of a farm wagon on the deck, too. The family all came to the open deck to see the showboat, except for the father, who handled the steering oar.

"Ahoy, there!" called the flatboat owner. "Is that flag right? You give shows on that boat?"

"Right," called Papa Chapman. "We shall be tying up at the river landings between here and New Orleans, every twenty miles or so. We shall take the finest entertainment to the frontier."

The flatboat family smiled and waved as they drifted on past the showboat.

A keelboat, fastest of the riverboats other than those

with steam power, was gaining on the showboat and the flatboats, too. It carried a load of freight bound from Pittsburgh to New Orleans, but would get there well ahead of the other boats because its rounded bottom above the square keel would move swiftly through the water. Its crew were all tough, seasoned riverboatmen. They had been loading freight at the docks at Pittsburgh when the showboat shoved off. The men waved greetings as they went by.

At noon, the showboat was not far below Pittsburgh.

"We'll have to make this boat go faster if we are going to travel twenty miles a day," Papa said.

The boatman who worked for him said, "Too much wind in the morning after the sun is high, Mr. Chapman. If you don't mind getting up early, we would do better before sun-up."

From then on, they moved the boat in the quiet hours after three o'clock in the morning, and finished their day's rest with the boat tied at the landing where the next show would be given.

Harry was the first to spot the black clouds of smoke that meant a steamboat was coming. It was gaining on the showboat at a fast rate. He pointed it out to Sarah, who sat on the deck shelling peas for dinner.

"Hoot! Hoot! Hooo-ooot!" came a throaty call from the steamboat whistles.

Harry began to wave, thinking it was a friendly greeting.

"Hoot! Hoooo-ooooot! HOOOOO-OOOOOOT!"

This time, it didn't sound as friendly. Harry saw boatmen on its upper deck waving off to one side. He ran back to his grandfather.

"Grandpa! We've got to move over! The steamboat is going to run right into us!" he cried.

It did look that way for a minute more. And then the showboat, which had been taking a nice course down the middle of the river, began to nose a little towards the shore. The steamboat needed the deepest part of the river in which to run. Its pilot, steering from the upper cabin with a big wheel that turned the boat's rudder, knew that he would go aground on a sandbar if he pulled nearer to the shore.

The boatman leaned hard on the steering oar. The steamboat was coming too close for comfort.

"Push on those poles, boys!" he yelled.

"HOOOT, HOOOT! HOOT, HOOO-OOOOT!"

The Chapman boys saw the big boat bearing down on them just in time to pull in their poles. With only

45

inches to spare, the big side paddle wheels churned past them. The sound of the engines was deafening. Then the steamboat was ahead of them and the showboat was rocking in its wake.

"Enough to make a body seasick," said Mama Chapman from the doorway of the living quarters. Then she went back inside to her cooking as if the sights of the river were already everyday things.

Soon they had really become everyday things. The days settled into a pattern. The showboat was usually tied at its new landing an hour or two before noon. Then, while the women got the noon meal ready, George and William would go ashore to let people know of the show that was coming, just as the Drake Players had done. Often William, seeing an easier way than to go around town all afternoon himself, would ask who might be hired to help out.

"Do you know anyone who can toot a horn like this?" he would ask. When someone was pointed out to him, he would hire the man, hang a sandwich board over his shoulders, and have a walking, horn-tooting advertiser all afternoon. The posters all told of how welcome ladies would be in the theater.

At seven-thirty, all of the family except Papa took

horns and fiddles and climbed the ladder to the showboat roof. When they began to play, it took a strong
will to keep anyone from coming down to the riverfront to see what was going on.

Papa Chapman stood at the end of the gangplank,
taking in the money. It cost fifty cents for a grownup
to see the show and twenty-five cents for a child.
Sometimes instead of money, he took in potatoes or
eggs or perhaps a chicken. A peck of potatoes, two
gallons of canned fruit or a side of bacon would get
two children or one adult into the theater.

Phoebe usually sang a free sample song or two.

"Come inside to hear more warbling from this
sweetest of songbirds," Papa Chapman called out to
the people. The players all moved inside then and
continued their concert in front of the stage. More
people were sure to make up their minds then to see
what was going on in the floating theater.

Papa pulled out his big pocket watch and looked
at it.

"Last call for the big show! Eight o'clock! Show
time!" he called out. As he stooped to pull in the
gangplank, there was always someone who hurried up
at the last moment.

Papa's eight o'clock call was the signal for the boys inside to light the candle footlights. The audience part of the theater had been lighted just before the concert began. From the center of the ceiling hung a round frame like a wagon wheel. On it were candles. There was almost always an empty seat or two on the benches right under the lighting fixture, for each person who sat there soon learned that he would have candle wax dripping onto him all evening.

Then at last came the moment of quiet when someone backstage gave the first tug at the curtains. The audience was instantly still, watching for the first sight of the stage setting. The curtains parted and the play was on. The stars were usually William Chapman, Jr. and his pretty young sister, Caroline.

After a number of weeks of this life, the Chapman family had everything timed perfectly. William became fond of using all his spare time fishing off the roof of the theater.

"This is the life for me," he said to Harry one lovely late summer evening. The two of them were lying on their backs on the roof, dangling fish lines into the Mississippi River in hopes a catfish would bite. They had just had their supper. Soon the people of Friar's

Point, Mississippi, would be leaving their homes to come down to see the show, but for the moment there seemed to be no hurry.

After a while, they heard Mama call, "Come, boys! Time to get dressed."

The two tied their poles to the low rail at the edge of the roof, leaving their lines in the water. In a few minutes they were back on the roof, in costume. They joined the family for the band concert. William had some free time then before his part in the show began, so he hurried back to his fish line.

Down in the theater, the footlights were lighted and the curtain parted. They were doing *The Stranger* that night, and William had the part of "Francis," while Papa Chapman played "the stranger." The play started with "the stranger" alone on the stage. Papa came to the place where he was to call to Francis to join him.

"Francis!" he called.

No Francis came onto the stage.

"Francis! *Francis!*" called Papa.

He looked hopefully towards the door where William was supposed to enter the stage.

Again he called, a little louder. Again he waited.

The audience began to murmur, wondering what was wrong.

"FRANCIS!" he shouted, and this time it was not "the stranger" calling, but William Chapman, Sr., angrily calling his son.

Away off came the answer, "Coming, sir!"

The audience could hear thumping noises on the roof above their heads. "The stranger" walked back and forth on the stage, hands behind his back, mouth set in an angry line, looking up at the ceiling.

Then in came "Francis." "Here I am, Sir."

Papa said, "Why didn't you come when I called?" The line was not in the play.

"Francis" said, "Why, Sir, I was just hauling in the biggest dog-gone catfish you ever saw in your life!"

The audience shouted with laughter. It was several minutes before the play could go on.

So the days went by. Late in the fall, the boat had floated all the way down to New Orleans. It was time to take out all the family's goods and pack them into chests. The boat itself had to be torn apart and sold for lumber. There was no way to move a big flatboat such as that was up the many miles of river.

The actors took their trunks and boxes to the steamboat landing and had a pleasant trip back up to Pittsburgh on one of the big double-decked steamboats. There they ordered another showboat built and settled down to wait for spring to come.

"It seems foolish to tear down the theater each year," he said. "Now if we could only buy ourselves a little steamboat, the steamboat could push the showboat back up the river. We could take sidetrips up some of the deep rivers that flow into the Ohio and the Mississippi, too."

In five years, they had enough money to buy the steamboat. By then, people were looking forward to the coming of the showboat each year. Someone would see it coming down the river, and the cry would go out, "Showboat's comin'!"

Then people for miles around would hitch Old Dobbin to the wagon and head for town. It was the big day of the year. There were other showboats besides the Chapman boat after a while, but none with better actors, or with a finer floating theater.

The Chapman family rode the rivers until 1847. By that time, the showboat had become an important part of American life.

Tom Rice, Father of the Minstrel Show

Each year, there were more steamboats churning the waters of the Ohio and the Mississippi with their great paddle wheels and filling the air with smoke and sound. The riverfronts of cities, such as St. Louis, Louisville and Cincinnati, had lines of the great double-decked boats, loading and unloading goods and people. Steamboats brought business. Business brought more people, and more people meant good business for the theaters.

Noah Ludlow found his "Ark" too old-fashioned in the day of steam-pushed showboats. He opened a theater in Louisville, Kentucky. One of Noah's property boys was a tall, lanky lad name Tom Rice.

Tom had stage fever too badly to be a property boy for long. When Noah's acting company could not use him as an actor, he went to Sam Drake. Sam saw that this young man had a special talent for making people laugh.

"Get out there in front of the curtain, Tom, and tell some of your stories while we set the stage for the next play," Old Sam told the boy.

Tom Rice stepped out and faced the audience. By this time they were growing restless and beginning to throw peanut shells. They stopped shelling peanuts to laugh at Tom's first joke. When he ran out of jokes, he broke into a jig dance. Tom was enjoying this so much himself that he was sorry when Old Sam poked him through the curtain as a signal that the stage was ready.

Tom often slept late in the morning after a long evening at work in the theater. Then, after his breakfast, he would walk down to the riverfront. He liked to hear the Negroes singing at their work of carrying bales and boxes onto or off the steamboats.

Negroes had been brought to America to work as slaves on the great plantations of the south. For many years, they made their lives a little brighter by singing together in a way that was all their own.

Some of the Negroes did other work now, such as working at the docks. But they brought with them their love of singing, and some of the songs of the southland. They had learned to make stringed musical instruments to bring out the beat of their songs, particularly the "banjar" which became the banjo. When a worker had a little time to wait for a steamboat, sometimes he would strum on his banjo and a little group would gather and sing.

Tom Rice listened and watched. His own feet would be tapping before he knew it, for he had the same urge to dance and sing. In his between-acts bits, he used some of the songs and dances he learned on the riverfront.

One sunny autumn day, Tom was in Cincinnati and looking for work.

"I'll have to let some of you go," Old Sam had said. "Seems more folks will go to the museum here than to the theater. Why a wax dummy or a stuffed animal is more interesting than a good comedy, I'll never understand. But I've got to close the show."

Before he gave up and left Cincinnati, Tom looked around for an opening. Finding none, he decided to go to Pittsburgh. He was walking down a block or two from his hotel looking for someone to carry his trunk down to the steamboat. He walked to the livery stable. There he saw an old Negro working at rubbing down the horses.

"Poor old fellow," Tom thought. "He's so much in

pain from aches in his joints that he shouldn't have to work at all."

But just then Tom saw the bent old man do a little dance step. Then he kicked up his heels and jumped into the air. Tom went closer and he could hear the old man singing a rather sad little tune. Again he saw the old man "set his heels a-rickin'". This time he was close enough to hear the words of the little song.

Turn about an' wheel about, and do jis so —
An' every time I turn about, I jump Jim Crow!

At the "jump Jim Crow" came the strange shuffling of the feet and the leap into the air with the heels tapped together.

Tom left Cincinnati as he had planned, but he could not forget the little tune and the dance step. He tried it out himself on the steamboat as he went upriver, making up verses to sing before the Jim Crow rhyme. In his hotel in Pittsburgh he finished the act, and decided he would use it at the first chance he got.

He was hired as an actor, and again was to do "bits" between acts. Here was his chance to "Jump Jim Crow." He went down to the sidewalk before theater time and looked around outside the hotel. A poor Negro was standing out there, with his mouth wide open as he leaned against the wall. There was a small crowd gathered near. One young man stood facing him, staring at the Negro's mouth.

"You can do it, Al," said one of the others.

"Five cents says he can't," said another.

Al said, "Hold still, Cuff. If I get a penny in your mouth, it's yours, you know."

Cuff stood very still. Al tossed the penny and it landed on Cuff's tongue. Cuff grinned as he took the penny from his mouth and put it into a purse he took from the pocket of his ragged coat.

"You wins, Mr. Al, and so do I," he said.

Tom Rice couldn't help feeling sorry for the poor fellow. He knew that Cuff earned part of his living in this way. The rest he earned by carrying trunks to and from the steamboat landing a short distance away. Tom stepped up to Cuff.

"Cuff, you can make a lot more money than you make letting them pitch pennies at you if you will come with me."

"What does I have to do, Massa Rice?" Cuff asked.

Rice took hold of Cuff's arm and led him towards the back entrance to the theater. He couldn't walk the man very fast because the soles of Cuff's shoes flapped so badly that Cuff almost tripped with each step. His trousers were several sizes too large and held up with a twist of rope. The coat never had matched the trousers, but that was hard to tell because both coat and trousers were covered with patches. On his head, Cuff wore an old straw hat, droopy of brim and torn.

"All you have to do is wait backstage while I do an act," Tom told Cuff.

"But Massa Rice, I gotta go down to the steamboat landin' before long," said Cuff. "A steamboat will be comin' in, and I gotta bring up a trunk to the hotel."

"It won't take long, Cuff," said Tom. "Then you can go down to the steamboat landing. I'll pay you as much as you would make carrying a trunk, anyway."

They were in a backstage room by then. Rice gave Cuff a big towel and said, "Here, Cuff. Take off your clothes and have them ready for me. You can wrap yourself in this while I use your clothes."

Cuff stared at Rice. He could hardly believe his ears. Why would Massa Rice want his ragged old clothes? But he did as he was told.

Between the acts, Rice hurried to Cuff. He put on a black wig made of curled moss, blackened his face and hands with burnt cork, and then got into the patched coat and trousers and the flappy shoes and hat. He hurried out to do his act, working in front of the curtains. As he came into sight, he bent over like the old man.

In the pit, the little orchestra played a bit of a jig tune and then began the new tune that Rice had taught them.

Half-talking, half-singing, Rice said,

"Oh, Jim Crow's come to town as you all must know,
An he wheel about, he turn about, he do jis so,
An every time he wheel about, he
JUMP JIM CROW!"

He looked so odd as he "set his heels a-rickin' " that the audience burst into laughter. They quieted to hear the next verse of his catchy little song. It was one he had made up about one of the Pittsburgh people they all knew. Then came the chorus with the little dance step.

"First on de heel tap, den on de toe,
Every time I wheel about I jump Jim Crow.
Wheel about and turn about and do jis so,
And every time I wheel about, I jump Jim Crow!"

He went on to verse after verse. The audience laughed harder with each one. The stage was ready behind him, but even the manager could see it would be foolish to stop Tom Rice while he had them held so well. Tom was enjoying himself, too.

He hardly heard the loud whisper that came to him from the place where the edge of the stage met the curtain.

"Massa Rice, Massa Rice — must have my clothes!"

Tom went on with another verse. The whisper became a voice.

"Massa Rice, Massa Rice! Must have my clothes. Steamboat's a-comin'!"

Rice went on. He was getting an even louder laugh than before, but he didn't know it was because a worried looking face was now in sight at the edge of the stage. This time Cuff called louder.

"Massa Rice! Massa Rice! *Must* have my clothes! Steamboat's a-comin' right now!"

Rice saw Cuff then, but waved him back. He couldn't let go of so good an audience. But Cuff would be held off no longer. Out he came onto the stage, right up to Tom.

"Massa Rice, give me my things! Gotta go *now* —

STEAMBOAT'S A-COMIN'!"

With one last wave, Tom let Cuff drag him offstage. As he gave the poor man his clothes, Tom could hear the whistles and clapping out front. His little act had been a big hit.

From then on, Tom Rice worked on his Negro act more and more. He added more songs and jokes and dances until he had a full-length show worked out, with other actors to help him. From this grew a brand new kind of show, which came to be known as the *Minstrel Show*.

It was as purely American as the showboat. While the Chapman family was teaching inland America to look forward to the coming of the showboat, the minstrel idea swept the country and began to take the form it was to keep for many years.

It always began with a bit of music and a half circle of men, all but one in blackface. The blackface actors wore white trousers, striped bright-colored shirts and bright blue swallow-tail coats. In this way, they were very different from Tom Rice in his borrowed costume. But the singing, the dancing and the jokes were kept.

The half circle of men stood ready. The one not in blackface wore a simple black and white outfit, and

was always in the center. There came a special little
blaring of the trumpets and the audience was quiet.

The man in the center called out, "Gentlemen, be
seated!"

The half circle of men sat down, and the fun began.
The audience was held for an hour or two by the best
dancing and the catchiest tunes and sweetest singing
they had heard in a long time. Even the jokes seemed
extra funny. The "minstrels" had come to town.

Ralph Keeler, Minstrel Boy

The minstrels who played one night in 1850 in a hall in Toledo, Ohio, finished their show in great style and hurried back to their dressing rooms to clean the burnt cork off their faces and hands. Mr. Kunkel, owner of the company, heard a knock on his dressing room door.

"Come in," he called. He did not turn, but in the crinkled, wavy mirror he saw the door open slowly. The head of a boy peered into the room.

"Well, come in or be on your way, boy," said Kunkel. He turned to see the boy better. About thirteen years old, he judged, and has a bad case of minstrel fever.

The boy came into the dressing room. By the time he had closed the door behind him, Mr. Kunkel had turned back to the mirror. He was greasing his neck to clean off the burnt cork. Some of the black had rubbed onto his high-buttoned underwear, blending into its grayness. But the boy did not notice the shabbiness of the little dressing room or the dirtiness of Mr. Kunkel's underwear. His eyes were bright, and he did not take them from Mr. Kunkel's face.

"Well?" said Mr. Kunkel after a moment. "Speak up, boy. What do you want?"

The boy found his voice. "The show, Mr. Kunkel. It was wonderful. I want to be a minstrel. Can I join your company?"

Mr. Kunkel eyed his young visitor. "What's your name, boy? Can you dance? Can you sing? What company have you been with?"

The questions stopped the boy for a moment. He swallowed hard. Then he said, "I've been working on lake steamers for some time. I am self-supporting, and my name is Ralph Keeler. I just finished a season on the steamer *Northern Indiana,* as keyboy."

"Yeah? But can you dance or sing or play the banjo? That's what we need in a minstrel show, not somebody to keep the actors' keys!"

Ralph drew himself up as tall as he could. It was very unhandy sometimes, to be small for your age. After all, he was almost a man and had been on his own for more than two years.

"The work of a keyboy, sir, is not taking care of keys. It is seeing to the comfort of the passengers in many ways." Then Ralph's tone changed. "Mr. Kunkel, please let me try to learn to be a minstrel. There's nothing in all the world I want to do more than that. Your show is wonderful. I think I can do some of the dance steps already."

He did a little jig step he had seen done on the stage. Kunkel looked at him as he wiped the grease from his hands onto a well-blackened towel. "That's pretty good, boy. But we're all filled up for this year. Tell you what, son. You learn to dance and play a banjo a bit, and we'll see you next year."

Ralph's hopes had gone flying high. They came crashing to earth again. A year! It seemed a lifetime. But — already he saw himself on the stage and heard the audience clapping as he took a bow. Mr. Kunkel was putting on his clothes. He had no more to say.

"I — I'll be seeing you next year, Mr. Kunkel. Goodby," Ralph said, and left.

He went home to his rooming house and went to bed. There was school the next morning, and he would need to be up early, but he could not sleep. When he had left the *Northern Indiana,* about two weeks ago, he had decided to use his savings to put himself through another year of school. But now the time in school seemed to be wasted. He must begin to practice to be a minstrel. When Mr. Kunkel came back, he would be as good as that boy they all talked about, Johnny Diamond.

After school the next day, Ralph stopped at an iron-worker's shop. He borrowed a drill and cut holes in the center of two of the "lucky" pennies he had been carrying for two years. He screwed these into the heels of his only pair of boots. They would have to do for dancing shoes.

He clicked the coppers as he walked to a second-hand store near the waterfront. He had seen a banjo in the window there.

"I need that banjo," he told the shopkeeper. But he had to settle for one from the back of the shop. Its rim was cracked and dirt had blackened its sheepskin face, but it was all he could afford. With the fine feel of the banjo under his arm and the satisfying click of his heels, he hurried to his second-story room.

He had been busy only a few minutes and the jig step seemed to be coming just right. The "Juba," it had been called on the minstrel program. But when he stopped dancing for a moment, there came a pound-ing on the floor from the room below.

"The landlady is using the broom handle again," Ralph sighed. "I suppose she doesn't like my dancing."

A bellowing voice came up through the floor. "Stop that noise!"

Ralph decided to try out his banjo. He'd have to dance when she wasn't home or find another place to practice. Playing the banjo didn't come nearly so easily as dancing. The sounds he made weren't music even to Ralph, who was easily pleased.

The next afternoon he danced again. This time the landlady came to his door. "Quit that racket or get out," she said. "I'll not have my floors ruined and my ears, too."

Ralph drew himself up as tall as he could. He would find another room, where people were not so fussy.

He rented a room over a tavern. He was sure the gay people who came there would like the sound of his dancing and music. He practiced in the daylight hours right after school, when there were not many people in the tavern. Even so, the owner told him he would have to stop.

There was a girl in Ralph's class at school who smiled at him often. Ralph took his banjo to school to show it to her and told her he needed a place to practice playing it and learning his dances.

"My father has a woodshed with a board floor in it. Why don't you come home with me and practice there?" the girl asked.

Each day then, Ralph went home with the girl. She sat in the woodshed with him. At first she listened to his playing and watched his dancing with a look on her face that pleased Ralph a great deal. But after several days, when Ralph thought he was getting better, she seemed bored. She even yawned in the middle of his song.

"Excuse me," she said. Then she added, "Ralph, can't you play something else?"

"I thought you liked *Jordan*," he said in a hurt tone.

"I did, — the first time. But you've played it and played it and played it. And you don't get all the notes right, Ralph."

Ralph said, "Guess I've got to go home now. Goodby."

The next day, he saw the girl smiling at another boy. After school she was at the new boy's side when Ralph was ready to walk home with her for another practice time in the woodshed.

"Not today, Ralph," she said. "Some other time — maybe."

Ralph felt blue for a while. Then he got an idea that seemed wonderful to him. He would train his own minstrel company, with just boys and forget the girls. He didn't need any girl.

Soon he had gathered about him the future *Young Metropolitans*. Ralph talked six boys into joining him. First he asked for all the money they could spare. With their money and some of his own, he bought three sets of bones, which were held between the fingers and shaken in rhythm. He added a triangle of steel to make a ringing note, a tambourine for its fine jingling and a cheap second-hand accordion. With the banjo this would be all the *Young Metropolitans* needed.

"We'll practice up in my room," Ralph said. He began writing out the jokes for his minstrel show and found the work so interesting that he decided not to go back to school. When the other boys came up after school, he was all ready to direct them in the show.

The boy who said he could play an accordion picked it up and tried it. The sound that came out was very wheezy.

"You'll have to practice some at home," he told the

player. "The show opens with a musical number that you'll have to play."

The boy worked hard, but all he could learn to play was a tune he said was called *The Gum Tree Canoe*. None of the other boys knew it. It was sad and wheezy sounding, but Ralph didn't know what to do about it. He spent most of his time practicing a dance called *The Virginia Walk Around* while his minstrel boys tried to get the beat right.

"I'll get us a hall and we'll give a show soon," he told the boys. He hoped to get back the money he had spent by selling tickets to a show. Otherwise, he knew his savings would soon be gone and he'd have to go back to work. He had only two weeks' rent money left and a little for food.

At the end of the first two weeks, the landlord called him to one side.

"My customers complain about those noises, Ralph. I don't want to be mean to you, but I have to keep my customers happy."

The next week, he said, "There are fewer customers each night, boy. Now let's have no more of those noises from your room."

Ralph had to practice. The next week, the landlord locked him out of the room.

"I told you to quit that noise!" he yelled. "And you owe me two weeks' rent."

Ralph said, "I'll pay it all as soon as I give a show. Please, sir."

"There ain't going to be no show, and I can't live on promises, boy. You've driven my customers away. Now go away, and don't come back."

"But —" Ralph saw the look in his landlord's eye. "Yes, sir, I'll get my things and go. Yes, sir."

"You'll go and right now. I've locked your things in your room to try to get some of my money back in selling them."

Ralph begged, but it did no good. He turned away, with nothing but the clothes on his back. He was back where he had started from two years earlier, when he had first run away from his uncle's home in Buffalo, New York.

"Guess I'll have to go back to the steamers and look for work," he decided. "I won't go back to Buffalo."

He walked down to the lakefront. Lake Erie was choppy, and even on dry land Ralph felt a return of the old waves of seasickness that had made his work on the steamers so hard for him. Just then he heard the wailing hoot of the whistle of a steam locomotive. The railroad out of Toledo had been built less than ten years before, but it seemed to be doing more business each day. Maybe there would be a job for him on the railroad.

Ralph hurried to the little depot. Steam was hissing from the black and gold locomotive and smoke was still rising from its red painted high stack. Maybe he could catch the conductor before he left the train.

The conductor was still in a passenger car, and Ralph was glad to see that he had a kind face.

"You say you've worked on steamboats?" the conductor asked. "Know how to keep passengers happy?"

"Yes, sir," said Ralph, "I know just how to please them. That is what my work as keyboy was. And before that, I waited on table."

"Well, son, we can't pay you wages, but I'll let you go through our trains selling books and papers. All you make on the job will be yours to keep."

Ralph wasted no time. He found out where he could get papers and magazines at the lowest price, and was on the next train out of Toledo. He rode the trains all day, walking back and forth, showing people interesting titles in his magazines to get them to buy. He sold some of his magazines and papers more than once by picking up those that passengers left when they got off the train.

He was also supposed to carry a pail of water through the cars so that the passengers could have a drink. One summer day, a circus man was on board the train. Ralph could almost smell out show people. He had not for a moment forgotten his plan to become a minstrel player, and always sat down to talk with show people who rode on the train.

"I'm saving my money so that I can get into the minstrels," he told the circus man.

The man eyed him and motioned to Ralph to come closer.

"I'll let you in on a little money-making secret, son," he said. "Instead of taking water through the cars on hot days and nights, here's what you ought to do —"

Ralph smiled as the man whispered his secret. The next night, when he filled the water bucket he added some brown sugar and a kind of acid the circus man had told him about. When the train was on its way, he started through the cars, calling, "Lemonade, five cents a glass!"

People bought his "lemonade." Ralph watched their faces as they tasted it, and knew they didn't like it very well. After while a man said, "Son, please bring me some plain water."

"Oh, I'm sorry, sir," Ralph said. "There is no water on the train."

It was the truth, for he had made all the water into lemonade. The lemonade sales added a great deal to his savings. One night he made fifteen dollars.

Almost a year had passed since he had talked to Mr. Kunkel. Ralph was thinking about quitting so as to practice some more when something else helped him make up his mind. All over America, in the years between 1845 and 1855, people had been dying of a sickness called *cholera*. It spread fast. People said that the travelers took it from one city to another. Ralph was afraid of the illness and decided he did not want to be with travelers. He left the railroad and rented a room.

The first time he practiced his dancing, at which he had become quite good, his landlady called him downstairs.

"Ralph," she said, "I know you love to dance and and you are good at it. But those boots are hard on my floors. Now here is where I want you to do your dancing."

She took him into the parlor and unrolled a length of oilcloth on the floor over the rug. On it, Ralph could "Juba" all day.

Several of the people who stayed in the same house had been or were then in show business. One played the piano very well. There was a piano in the parlor, and often the man played while Ralph danced.

One evening, Ralph did not feel like dancing. His head ached.

"I am getting the cholera!" he thought with alarm.

He walked down the street to the St. Nicholas Hotel, and went into a room marked BAR. He felt unsure of himself as he looked around, for there were only grown men there. Some were at tables and some were standing at the long bar, leaning on the counter with one foot on the brass rail that was set about nine inches up from the floor.

Ralph walked over to the bar, put a foot on the rail and tried to put an elbow on the counter top. But he was too short.

"Bartender," he called. His voice squeaked in the middle of the word. He tried again and did better. "A good ten-cent drink of pale brandy," he said in his best deep voice. "And none of that instant death kind, either."

The bartender stared at the boy for a moment, not sure if he should give him the brandy. But once he had been roundly scolded by a midget who worked for a circus when he asked about his age. In those days there were no laws about who could be served at a bar. He brought the brandy.

Ralph made the mistake of swallowing too much of the fiery drink at once. He coughed and choked. The bartender gave him water to drink, and decided this was really a boy, not a short man.

"Sonny, you have no business drinking brandy or anything else we serve in here. Now, go home like a good boy."

Ralph had ordered the brandy only because he had heard someone say, "The best thing to do if you think you are getting cholera is to get a drink of brandy right away."

"Yes, sir," he said. "It tastes awful, anyway." Then he remembered the men in the room, most of whom were watching him. He tried to act as if he had often been at a bar as he tossed his dime onto the counter.

He was about to go when he heard a man at the nearest table say, "Who, for pity's sake, is that?"

Ralph could see, from the corner of his eye, that a man was turning to look at him. The man turned back quickly and Ralph heard him say, "Johnny, that's just the boy you've been looking for."

"Come over here, Ralph," the man called. Ralph knew the man. He was one who had come to the boarding house on a night when Ralph had been dancing in the parlor.

"I hear you can dance," said the man called Johnny.

"This is Johnny Booker, Ralph," said the other man.

Ralph's eyes nearly popped out of his head. Johnny Booker was a well-known minstrel man. There was even a song about him called, *Meet Johnny Booker in the Bowling Green.*

Johnny was saying, "I'd like to see you dance, boy."

Ralph forgot his headache. He forgot all about cholera. They went upstairs to Mr. Booker's room in the hotel. The minstrel singer clapped and whistled a tune and Ralph danced.

"You're hired," said Johnny Booker. "With some training, we may make another Johnny Diamond out of you. You have a feel for dancing. I'll give you five

dollars a week and your traveling expenses. Is it a deal?"

Ralph's head was swimming and not only from the brandy. Suddenly his big dream was coming true. He would be in a minstrel show. He didn't even think about the pay and he couldn't remember later how he got back to his room at the boarding house.

He began practicing with Mr. Booker the next day. Booker was waiting for some other men of his company to arrive before they went "on the road."

As others in the company came to Toledo, Ralph thought each one must be a big star. Some carried big oilcloth-covered bass viols, guitars or banjos. They all clapped Ralph on the shoulders after they saw him dance.

"You've made a find, Johnny," Ralph heard one of them say. It made him feel very good.

There was one thing unusual about the actors that Ralph noticed. They all kept their coats buttoned up, so he began to keep his buttoned, too. He thought it was a mark of the trade, and it wasn't until later, when they were on the road, that he learned the reason. It saved wear and tear on shirts. The men wore no shirts at all, only a pair of cuffs and the part of the shirt collar and front that showed above the coat.

Ralph was in heaven when the first show was given. People in the audience clapped and cheered for the small figure doing the fast-stepping dances. He even did one dressed like a girl, and had fun doing it. Then the new banners were made to hang across the main streets of the towns they visited. Ralph swelled with pride when he saw his picture painted on them.

He could look out of his hotel room window and see himself above the carriages and wagons that moved down the street. The picture showed him in the bright-colored flannel knee pants he wore for most of his dances, and the jacket with the gold braid on it that Johnny had bought for him. One leg and one arm were raised as he danced the "Juba."

BENEFIT was in big letters at one end of the banner. This meant that the show was being given to raise money for the boy. More people were willing to go to a show when they thought the money was being used to help an orphan boy. Ralph thought of the extra money he would get and did his very best in the show.

When the show had ended, he knew people liked him.

"How much money do I get?" he asked Johnny Booker.

"Your five dollars will be paid at the end of the week," said Johnny.

Ralph asked, "I don't mean that. I mean the money from the benefit for me."

Johnny laughed and roughed up Ralph's hair. "Oh, I thought you knew that benefit sign was just a come-on to bring in the money, Ralph. It's a trick of the trade. You'll learn."

Ralph learned. It didn't bother him too much, for he was in show business. He was an important part of a real minstrel company. He went onto the stage each night ready to dance his best. The audience always clapped and cheered. He was good, almost as good as Johnny Diamond.

Doc Spaulding, and the Floating Palace

Ralph Keeler learned more dances, and had fun doing it. He liked his trainer, Mr. Frank Lynch. Frank liked to talk about the days when he had been a performer in P. T. Barnum's circus.

"I was fourteen years old, Ralph," said Frank. "You remind me of myself as I was then. It was about the time you were born, or maybe a year or two later. I was an orphan boy, like you. I learned to dance the same way you did, by practicing the steps I saw others do. Then, when I joined Barnum, I was with Johnny Diamond. He taught me to really step lively."

With Frank's help, Ralph soon learned all the tricks of the trade that had made Johnny Diamond famous.

Sometimes Frank and Ralph would take time out for some fun. In good weather, they would go up to the roof of the hotel where they were staying.

"See those people walking along down there?" Frank asked on the first afternoon they did this. "Now I'll play a tune on the fife and you beat the drum. Watch what happens."

84

It was a warm day and people were in no hurry. Frank began with a slow beat, playing *The Girl I Left Behind Me,* slowing it down to the step of most of the people. Then he winked at Ralph and gradually played faster and faster. Ralph kept up the beat on the drum. When he looked down at the people he had to laugh. There they were, marching along in time to the music as if they were all in a hurry.

"That one fellow down there —" Frank said and pointed his fife at a man, "is paying no attention to the beat." He began to play again, this time making the music match the slow step of the one man. Soon almost all the people were changing their pace to stay with the beat.

"There. Now they are all in step," said Frank. "Now you and I can get to work."

After a few months, Johnny Booker, was worried. The audiences had not been so large lately, for times were a little hard. The company was in Pittsburgh when the end came. The hotel man locked the rooms with the actors' goods in them because the bills weren't paid.

"Come on, kid," Frank Lynch said to Ralph. "We'll stick together."

They began again, and soon there was a new company of Booker Minstrels. They were in Cincinnati, Ohio, in the spring of 1856 when the big circus showboat, the *Floating Palace* was tied up at the riverfront.

"Doc Spalding is getting his circus showboat company ready for a new season," Johnny Booker told the others. "I've signed us up to ride the rivers this summer."

Showboats had changed a great deal since the Chapman family had run the first one. Now they were great, two-story theaters, set onto a barge a little less clumsy than the old flatboats. A few had their own steam engines, but most of them were pushed up or down the river by a small steamboat. The showboats themselves were now as fine as any theater on the land.

The *Floating Palace* and its "tow," the steamboat *James Raymond,* were a little different from some of the others. Spalding & Rogers Circus Company had decided to have their circus shows on the boat, instead of having to unload everything from the boat in which they traveled and set up the tents on land. But the company also gave plays and minstrel shows. For all this, they needed many people, room to keep the circus animals, space in the showboat for the circus ring and swings and ropes for the acrobats, and a regular theater with a stage for the plays and minstrel shows.

They had all this and more on the *Floating Palace* and the *James Raymond*. Ralph and the others of Johnny Booker's company went down to see it. Ralph's eyes nearly popped out of his head.

"Boy, it sure is big!" he said.

Both boats gleamed with white paint. Along the sides of the showboat, in great red and gold letters, was painted FLOATING PALACE. The great banner flying from the mast on the roof carried the same words. At the bow flew the forty-starred American flag and a pennant. From the stern flew a red and gold flag with a horse and the Spalding & Rogers Circus Company name on it.

The owner, Dr. Spalding, had that title because he had learned the drug business and could mix medicines. He looked like a doctor, too, with his big mustache and pointed beard.

"We will go up to Pittsburgh this week, non-stop, and start giving our shows on the downriver trip," Doc Spalding told the company.

All the hundred or so people who helped run the boats or took part in the shows lived on board the

James Raymond. The dining hall was there, too, as well as a theater room that was more beautiful than any Ralph had ever seen.

Ralph had time to look around the two boats and see the show people and the circus animals come on board, and to see everything on the boats.

He saw the big auditorium on the *Floating Palace,* with its circus ring and stage. Gold painted chairs, cane-seated and bolted to the floor, were around the great room. These were the highest price seats, called the *dress circle.* Raised a little and behind the dress circle rows were the *family boxes,* with padded cushioned benches. The upper part of the room was a great gallery with the plain wooden seats that were lower priced. More than two thousand people could be seated in the auditorium at one time.

Ralph saw the forty beautiful, trained circus ponies and horses being brought on board. There were stables for them at the stern of the *Floating Palace,* and stable boys to take care of the fine animals.

Then came the circus people. Ralph stood at the rail of the *James Raymond,* watching them come on board with their boxes and chests of costumes and things they used in their acts. He wondered about one little family he saw. There was a man who looked like a lawyer, his quiet wife, their little girl and the nursemaid.

"That lady is Madame Olinda," Ralph was told. "She looks so quiet now, but you should see her dressed for her act. She walks that tight rope that you saw strung from one corner of the *Palace* gallery to the other. There is nothing to catch her if she falls. The big pipe organ in there booms out a note for each step she takes, and everyone in the place holds his breath."

Ralph asked, "Did she ever fall?"

"Almost did, once. Madame Olinda gave orders that her little girl was never to be in the auditorium while she was doing her act. Then, one day, she looked down and saw the child. She gasped, and fell. She dropped her balance pole, and somehow caught the rope and held on. You should have heard the screams of the people in the audience! Believe me, that nursemaid made sure that the little girl was never in there again when her mother's turn came to perform."

Ralph's attention was caught next by a man and woman who were having a little trouble. The lady walked with the spring that marked her as a dancer.

"Madame Leontine, trained in France," Ralph was

told. "Wife of the Professor there. Professor Thaddeus Lowe, magician. They do the *Invisible Lady* stunt in the museum, too."

Ralph had seen the brass ball with four trumpets on it in the museum room. He learned later that Madame Leontine went into a room beneath it, talked into a brass tube and answered questions asked by people who talked into the trumpets.

The "Professor" was a young man, in his twenties. He wore his hair long, in two braids down his back. He was having a great deal of trouble carrying luggage onto the boat and at the same time keeping a hold on the end of a chain in his hand. At the other end of the chain was a bear cub who clearly did not want to walk the gangplank.

"Go help him," Ralph was told, and Ralph hurried to the rescue, to take some of the bags and boxes from the Professor's arms.

"Thaddeus S. C. Lowe is the name," said the Professor. He bowed as well as he could under the load he carried. Then he turned to his bear cub. Ralph took boxes on board the boat and came back for more. Finally, with his arms free, the Professor picked up the sprawling cub and carried him on board.

"Keep that animal away from me, Professor," said one of the girl dancers.

The Professor kept a firm hold on the cub's chain, but he said, "Madame, if each person on board were as well behaved as this little animal, we should have no problems at all."

Captain William McCracken, master of the *James Raymond* did not mind having a bear on board. The fat, jolly captain was used to all manner of strange things about him.

"You can keep him in the gas room, Professor," he said. "Just see that he is chained, and he will be all right."

The gas room was the place in which a machine was kept which made the coal gas for the lights on the *Raymond* and the big *Floating Palace*. This was a full-time job for the young man who turned the crank on the machine, for the *Floating Palace* was lighted so brightly outside as well as inside that people came to see it at night even if they were not going to the show. The gas boy, luckily, took a liking to Bruno, the bear.

With a toot of its whistle and much clanging of bell signals from the pull cords in the pilot house of the *James Raymond,* the steamboat moved into position be-

hind the *Floating Palace*. The two boats were clamped together, and the upriver trip began. It was early April. Usually, spring rains had made the river deep by April, but this was a dry spring. Captain McCracken had soundings taken, and was disturbed to hear that there was less than ten feet of water in the deepest part. Three feet less than that, and they would be in trouble. Everyone hoped for rain to make the river rise.

Ralph soon became well acquainted with everyone on board the boat, and especially with the Professor and his wife. Madame Leontine gave Ralph lessons each day. He had to learn the dancing positions a

ballet dancer used, and learn them well, so that he could do a comic act of ballet. Madame Leontine kept a tiny whip in her hand, and gave Ralph's hands or feet a little flick each time he made a mistake. To make up for this, she also gave him plenty of praise when he did well.

In his free time, Ralph went to the gas room to play with Bruno. Sometimes the Professor was there, teaching the bear to obey and to do tricks. The Professor was very much interested in the workings of the gas machine, too.

"There ought to be a better way than that to make

gas for lighting," he said often. Then he would stare at the machine for a long time.

The rain did not come. The two boats were about twenty-five miles down the Ohio from Wheeling, West Virginia, and Captain McCracken had to keep the speed down and pick his way along the deepest part of the Ohio River. But early one morning came the sudden scraping sound that meant they had struck a sand bar. The big paddlewheels on the *Raymond's* sides churned the water, turning backward, but the boat would not move. The *Floating Palace* was still afloat, but the *Raymond* was hard aground.

"Everyone except the crew go on board the *Palace,*" ordered Captain McCracken. "That may lighten the load enough to get us off this bar."

With everyone on the showboat, the hooks were removed and the *Palace* separated from her tow.

"Drop anchor!" yelled Captain McCracken.

Before the *Palace's* anchors took hold, the big showboat had floated back downstream a half mile from the *Raymond.* Ralph and the others on board thought it would be only a short while until the *Raymond* freed itself and came down to get the *Palace.* All through the morning, they watched the work going on in the distance. There was no food on board the *Palace,* and by noon everyone was hungry.

"They'll send food down from the *Raymond,*" someone said.

To help him forget how hungry he was, Ralph went back to the museum for the really good look at things he had been planning to have for a long time. "Over 100,000 curiosities," the ads said. There were glass cases with everything from dressed fleas to swords from all the past wars. There were life-size wax figures, all the way from the Twelve Apostles to Napoleon. A few cages held small live animals, but most of the animals in the big room were stuffed. There was an alligator on the floor, looking ready to eat anyone who stubbed his toe on the open jaws. A stuffed giraffe bumped its head against the ceiling. There was a little stage for "Punch and Judy" puppet shows, and off in one corner was a printing press. There, Mr. McCreary, who had once worked on a big city newspaper, printed a daily newspaper to sell to the people who came to see the museum exhibits. The newspaper had wild stories about the past of the things in the museum, such as how many people the alligator had eaten and how he had finally been captured. Mr. McCreary also made and sold lemonade which reminded Ralph of the kind he had once sold on the train. He usually had ginger-bread for sale, too, but there wasn't even any of that for the people to eat because the showboat was not yet open for business.

The Professor and Madame Leontine wandered into the museum, too, with Bruno on his chain. While the Professor and his wife were showing Ralph how "The Invisible Lady" worked, Bruno was allowed to walk free. Ralph saw him biting into the fur of a stuffed chipmunk.

"Professor, look what Bruno is doing!" Ralph said.

The Professor took the cub by the collar and rapped him on the nose. But the bear, who always looked as if he were smiling, went on grinning and tried to get back to the chipmunk.

"No, no!" said Madam Leontine. "The poison is in the little animal. Not good, Bruno! Make you very, very seek!"

The afternoon wore by, and no food came from the *Raymond,* nor did the steamboat get free of the sand bar.

"I cannot live another hour without food," moaned

the fat bass singer, Riesse. He had been wailing for food since noon.

About dark, a cheer went up. The skiff was seen coming from the *Raymond.*

"Here they come with a boatload of food for us!" cried Riesse.

The small boat arrived, with Captain McCracken and two others, but they had brought no food. They had forgotten about such matters as food for all the people.

"Too dark to make another trip," said the Captain.

The people stretched out wherever they chose to lie in the boat. Ralph chose the floor of the museum, but he was sorry later, for Riesse was there, too. Ralph, lying between the case that held the Twelve Apostles and a wax figure of Robert Burns, listened to the groanings and wailings of the hungry singer until early morning. Then at last he dropped off to sleep.

Daylight came. The *Raymond* was still stuck, and several other steamboats were stuck, too. The river water had dropped even lower. The skiff returned to the *Palace.* Captain McCracken had hired a small steamer to take his people on board, get them some food, and then take a few days' tour, giving small shows. Until it rained, the *Palace* was out of business.

A week later, they were finally on their way upstream again. The long awaited rains had come, and the Ohio rose enough to float the steamboats.

Bruno had enjoyed his visit to the museum so much that he made a daily visit there, and was often found taking a bite or two of a stuffed animal.

"It is a wonder he doesn't get sick on the poison used in stuffing those animals," Mr. McCreary said. "Aside from that, Professor, I wish you would keep him out of here. I've already had to throw out several exhibits he chewed up."

"But he is so cute!" said one of the dancers who liked the bear. "He would not hurt anyone. It is cruel to keep him chained up in the gas room all the time."

"He should never be running loose," others said. "He might decide to bite someone any day. He is growing bigger all the time."

The people began to line up on two sides, friends of Bruno and enemies of Bruno. At the dinner table, Bruno was the main thing talked about.

"Just look at what he did to this wig!"

"Chewed the toe out of one of my best boots!"

The drummer reported, "He bit a hole in my drum."

They all looked at the Professor.

"Now you know I'll make good on all he did," the Professor said. But Captain McCracken saw the trouble ahead.

"He's a good little fellow, Professor, but keep him locked up, please. There are too many things happening."

But the next day, Bruno broke his chain. He got into the dressing room of a minstrel man and chewed holes in the red and yellow striped pants the man wore for his part in the show. Again the dinner table buzzed with talk.

"Oh, he's just playful," said one of Bruno's friends.

"Playful? You call that playful?"

One woman said, "Why, I heard of a bear that ate forty children. I don't call that exactly playing."

Captain McCracken said, "Professor, you'll have to padlock the gas room."

"I will," said the Professor. "But Bruno hasn't bitten anyone. And I don't think he did all of the things for which he is blamed."

The people all took sides. The enemies of Bruno did not seem satisfied even when Bruno stayed locked in his room for several days. They went to the gas

room in the middle of the night, pried open the padlock and threw it away, and then cut Bruno's chain
to make it look as if he had broken loose. They made
Bruno come out of the gas room, pushed him to the
edge of the deck and into the river.

The next morning, the Professor came storming to
the breakfast table. "Someone cut Bruno's chain.
Where is he?"

The enemies of Bruno looked at one another. "You
mean Bruno is gone? How very, very sad. We'll all
miss the poor little fellow. Maybe he drowned himself
in shame for all the things he did."

At noon, Ralph heard a whining sound near the
stern of the *Floating Palace* as he was about to jump on
board the *Raymond.* He looked down into the river,
and caught sight of a bit of wet fur, almost hidden
under the stern of the showboat.

"Professor! Professor Lowe, come here!" he called.

The Professor came running. By this time, Ralph
could see Bruno, clinging to the rudder of the *Floating
Palace.*

"I'll help you get him on board," he said. A few
more friends of Bruno came to help. Soon they had
the poor bear, wet of fur and sad of eye, but with the

grin still on his face, back in the gas room. The Professor fed him and dried him. He put a new padlock on the door and gave one key to the boy who worked the gas machine and kept the other himself.

A night or two later, several enemies went into the museum. They took the wax figure of George Washington from his horse and sat him on the alligator. They put a battered old hat onto the head of beautiful Helen of Troy.

In the morning, one of them said to Mr. McCreary, "Did you see what that bear did to your museum?" But Mr. McCreary was a friend, and he knew that the bear could not have done this.

"You'll have to be smarter than that," he said.

Several days went by in which a sad, quiet Bruno stayed in the gas room except at show time when the Professor had him doing simple tricks.

Then one morning, a frontiersman came on board the *Raymond*. Such men often came to the riverboats selling wild game for meat.

"I have some nice bear steaks for sale," said the frontiersman.

The Professor, standing near by, turned without a word and ran for the gas room. It was a known fact that bears were no longer commonly found on the frontier near the rivers. In a minute, the Professor was back, angry and shouting.

"Bruno is gone! Someone broke the padlock, cut his chain and let him out. What is more, I am sure he was driven off this boat. He wouldn't go that far by himself!"

He walked up to the hunter and grabbed the front of the man's hunting shirt.

"Where did you shoot that bear?" he yelled into the man's face.

The man did not know what to think of this madman. He could hardly speak for fright. "R-right near the river, on my farm."

"Why did you shoot him? Was he hurting you?" the Professor shouted and shook the poor man.

"My-my dogs woke me up, barking and yelping the way they used to do when they had treed a bear," said the frontiersman. "Naturally, I took my gun and went after him. I didn't know he wasn't wild, mister. Honest I didn't."

The Professor loosened his hold. The man couldn't be blamed for the work of the enemies, and it was too late now. He turned away sadly. Later he learned that he had been right about Bruno having been forced off the boat. The enemies had even thrown sticks and stones at him to make him run away.

Ralph missed Bruno almost as much as the Professor did. The boy in the gas room looked very lonesome, too. The Professor stayed in his stateroom all morning and did not come to dinner.

Ralph wished he had not come to dinner, either, for on his plate was a slice of bear steak. He and the other friends did not eat a bite of meat, but the enemies chewed it up and smacked their lips.

"Wonderful steak," said one. "Never tasted better."

Another said, "The only good bear is a dead bear. . . ."

Then Mr. McCreary got to his feet. "Ladies and gentlemen, I speak for your own good," he said. "I wish to remind you of one of the strange habits of the late Bruno. Men of science would be surprised that he lived as long as he did. You will recall that he was very fond of eating stuffed animals from my museum. It should have killed him long ago. The poison in those animals must have been stored in Bruno's body. I am sure he ate enough to kill twenty men."

Several of those who had been eating bear steak

with great enjoyment now laid down their knives and forks.

"It will be a matter of interest to see if the poison shows up in any way in those who ate the meat," Mr. McCreary went on. "Kindly report any illness to me."

Mr. McCreary sat down. The friends of Bruno grinned at him. Already, several enemies had left the table. Not one more bite of bear meat was eaten. The cook had to throw all that was left of the meat into the river.

In the days that followed, the shows went on as usual, once in the afternoon and once in the evening. But the Professor was seldom seen between shows. Ralph went looking for him one day. He found him in the gas room, sewing together some pieces of fine cloth.

"What are you doing, Professor?" Ralph asked. He had thought that the Professor would be sitting staring at Bruno's broken chain, as some said he now did all day.

"I am not only going to make a better gas machine than this one," the Professor said. "In the meantime, I am going to make a balloon, and the day will come when I will fill it with a gas lighter than air and make a longer balloon journey than anyone has yet taken."

He explained to Ralph how a balloon would rise if it were filled with heated air, but that it came down when the air cooled. His study of gas had made him sure that special gases could do a better job of making it possible for man to fly through the air.

It was soon afterward that the Professor began going up into the air in a basket attached to a big balloon. He left the *Floating Palace* to work on his new idea.

Ralph missed him. He was growing tired of the show business that had seemed so wonderful to him not long before, too. There were other things in life that seemed to matter more. He had an offer to join one of the very best of minstrel shows, but he talked it over with Captain McCracken.

"Captain, if I go to New York to take that offer, I'll stay in show business all my life, I suppose. I don't think that is what I want. I can't forget how it felt to be locked out of a hotel room when business was too bad to get enough money to pay the rent. And look at Frank Lynch. He once was a dancer, just like me."

Frank, who had helped Ralph so much, had grown fat and sick. He could no longer dance, and it was hard to find a place for him in the work of running a show.

"Remember that school we saw near the river below St. Louis, Captain? Do you suppose I could go there?"

The Captain was sure Ralph could go to the school. In the months that followed, he and the showboat people slipped all the money they could spare into Ralph's purse to help him.

He said good-by to all of them one day and settled down to study. He worked hard and became a newspaper man and a writer. It was one of his books that told much about life on a showboat.

While Ralph was in school, the War Between the States began. It brought an end to the show days of the Spalding boats. The *Floating Palace* was in New Orleans when the war began. It was put to work as a hospital ship for southern soldiers. The *James Raymond* went to work for the northern armies, carrying troops and supplies. The money that Doc Spalding and Mr. Rogers were paid for the steamboat was sent back to President Lincoln to be used to help wounded men and the families of those killed in the fighting.

The Professor, Thaddeus Lowe, had, by that time, learned to use gas in his balloon. Just as the War

Between the States began, he made a balloon trip that set a new record for time and distance. He proved that photographs could be taken in the air, even in those days when the camera was a new invention. He went to President Lincoln with his ideas and was made "Chief of Aeronautics of the United States Army." From his balloon, he followed the movement of troops and was of help to the United States. Someone called him, in later times, the "One Man Air Force." He went on with his work with gas and invented the best way to make gas for home lighting. It was used until electricity came into houses.

After the War Between the States, showboats sailed the rivers once again, following for many years in the wake of the pioneer floating theaters.

Annie Oakley and the Wild West

In the years of the War Between the States and right afterward, a little girl named Annie Moses was growing up near Greenville in western Ohio. Seventy years had passed since the great Indian council had been held there, after "Mad" Anthony Wayne's battle with the Indians that had opened western Ohio for settlement. But even after seventy years, there were still dark woods and unplowed fields around Annie's home.

Annie took her dead father's rifle from its rack on the wall when she was no taller than the rifle. Soon she learned to shoot well enough to get rabbits and wild fowl for meat for her family. Before long, she was able to shoot more than her family needed, and she had some to sell.

A neighbor told her, "Annie, the hotels down in Cincinnati will always buy good quail to serve in their dining rooms. They pay a high price. I'll take yours to market for you."

That day was the beginning of a new life for Annie

Moses, the first step that would make her "Annie Oakley of the Wild West," and would take her to many parts of the world. She hunted so much that she became a "crack" shot. She could hit a quail at a long distance, neatly through the head. She shipped the birds, wrapped in cool, wet marsh grasses, down to Cincinnati.

"I'll take all that little hunter girl will send me," said the manager of the hotel that bought the birds. "My customers don't like to find shot in the meat they are eating. Annie Moses' birds never have shot anywhere but in the head."

By the time Annie was sixteen, she could follow a bird as it rose into the air, sight along the barrel of her old rifle and bring the bird down with never a miss. She spent all her time tramping the fields and woods and marshes around her Darke County home.

Then, one day, a letter came from her older sister, who had married and gone to live in Cincinnati.

"Come and live with Joe and me, Annie," her sister wrote. "It is time you saw a life beyond those woods. I will teach you to read and write, and the other things a young lady should know."

Annie was afraid to go to the city, but her mother

knew it was best for the girl. Cincinnati was the "Queen City of the West" in those days, and Mrs. Moses thought it too good a chance for Annie to miss.

In a few days, Annie was there. Her sister and brother-in-law began showing her the wonderful buildings and the great avenues. She saw the fine houses high on the hills, the busy riverfront with its steamboats, the canalboats snaking their way down to the river, and the puffing steam locomotives. She saw the fine hotels where people ate the quail she had shot, the splashing waters in the fountain in the square, and the horsecars that took people about the city. It was a whole new world for Annie.

Joe, her brother-in-law, took her to the shooting galleries one evening. Target shooting was a favorite sport in Cincinnati then. After he had practiced a little, Joe handed Annie a rifle.

"Like to try it?" he asked.

Annie held the gun a moment, getting its feel. It was much shorter than her father's old rifle. Then she began to shoot.

"Ping, ping, ping, ping, ping!" rang the bell in the target.

"Five shots and she hit it each time!" Joe stared at

this little sister-in-law of his. She stood barely five feet tall and weighed no more than a hundred pounds. Yet she could shoot far better than he could. He had her try again and again. It seemed she couldn't miss. Down went the moving ducks, pop, pop, pop, pop.

"Say, miss," said Charlie, the man in charge of the gallery. "I'd like to see you shoot against Frank Butler."

"You mean the fellow who is putting on the shooting shows over at the Coliseum?" asked Joe.

"That's the one," said Charlie. "How about it, miss? Ever been on the stage?"

"Oh, no!" said Annie. "I've never been anywhere except Darke County."

"She shot a lot of quail up there," Joe explained. "I think she sent most of the birds to the Bevis House, here in Cincinnati."

Charlie's eyes held great respect. It was strange that a pretty little brown-haired girl should be the best shot that had ever come to his gallery, and he had heard about the fine quail at the Bevis House. "The fellow who runs that hotel is a pal of mine. He told me just today that he can't get that fine Darke County quail any more. Now I see why. He'd like to meet you. What's more, that's where Frank Butler is staying.

113

Come on, you two. I'll close up here and we'll go over to the hotel."

Frank Butler was not in when they reached the Bevis House, but the manager was very pleased to meet Miss Annie Moses, hunter from Darke County.

"Sure do miss those quail you sent me," he said rather sadly. "Tell you what. I'll be glad to set up a match with Frank when he comes in. I'll tell him it's against the hunter who has been sending the quail he always liked. He'll be surprised when he meets the little lady."

A few days later it was all arranged. There were several "hunting clubs" around Cincinnati in those days. Joe took Annie to one on top of one of the hills. The club members went there to practice shooting at round clay disks, called *pigeons,* that were shot into the air by a little machine.

Soon Annie found herself facing a handsome young man, with a shotgun resting easily in the crook of his arm. He took off his green felt hat with the feather in it, and bowed over her hand. Annie found herself, a moment later, looking into the bluest eyes she had ever seen.

"This is Miss Annie Moses, Mr. Butler," said the

hotel manager. "She's the quail hunter you are to shoot against."

Frank Butler dropped his hat in his surprise.

"This pretty young lady a hunter? Well, I'll be —"

A few minutes later the match was on. Annie had no chance to practice with the strange gun. She watched as Frank took his position for the first shot.

"Pull!" he called.

Up flew the bit of clay.

"Bang!" The clay was in bits.

"Dead!" called the referee.

Then it was Annie's turn. She had chosen the gun which seemed to feel best, although none of them were like Pa's old rifle. As she stepped up to the shooting line, her hands were shaking so that she could not shoot.

Joe saw how nervous she was. "Just remember they are *birds,* Annie," he whispered, and patted her on the shoulder. Annie steadied herself.

"Pull!" she called, and pointed the gun to follow the rising pigeon. Her finger pulled the trigger and in a moment came the call, "Dead!"

Frank and Annie took turns. They were to fire a round of twenty-five shots. Through twenty-four, the

count was even. Each clay pigeon that rose had been neatly shattered.

It was Frank's turn again. This time, the pigeon sailed to the ground, unbroken.

"A miss!" called the referee.

Annie took her place to fire. "Dead!" was the call a moment later. Frank Butler took her small hands in his big ones. There was a look of real respect in his eyes.

From then on, Annie and Frank worked together as a team. Annie had never liked her name of Moses. She chose a new one that sounded right to her, and she was Annie Oakley from then on, and as she and Frank began their traveling to theaters and shooting matches, the gun cases were marked with the name of their act, "Butler and Oakley." They gave shooting shows at towns all over the midwest, in Ohio, Indiana, Illinois, Michigan and Wisconsin. Between shows, Frank taught Annie to read and write.

A few months after they met, they were married. When people clapped much louder and longer for his little wife than for him, Frank didn't mind. After a while he let her do all the shooting, and became her manager. Annie learned to shoot backwards, over her shoulder, sighting a moving target in a mirror. She could shoot holes into the center of playing cards tossed into the air. "Little Sure Shot," she was called.

Annie was twenty-four years old, but still looked like a girl in her teens when another part of her life began. She and Frank had signed up to travel with the Sells Brothers Circus during the summer months. When fall came, Mr. Lewis Sells decided to take the circus down to New Orleans where a big fair was to be held. There were to be exhibits from all over the United States and from other countries, too. It was honoring the hundred years that Louisiana had been growing cotton and shipping it from the port of New Orleans.

Mr. Sells explained to his company his reasons for thinking it would be a good place for the circus to go. "They will be running special trains into the city all winter and are expecting many people to come. After people have seen the Fair, they will look for other things to do. Then they'll come to the circus."

At New Orleans, the Sells Brothers set up their great tent and their many smaller tents and animal cages on a field near the river at the edge of town. When the Fair opened, they were ready. Annie and Frank set up housekeeping in a small tent, and Annie practiced her shooting every day.

On the grounds of the race track on the other side of New Orleans, another show was set up. Its owner, "Buffalo Bill" Cody, had the same idea that Mr. Lewis Sells had. Buffalo Bill's days as an Indian scout and hunter were behind him then, for times had changed. Gone were the great herds of buffalo, and homesteaders' plows were breaking the soil of the plains. Many of the last great Indian tribes had been cut down to almost nothing by fighting and by the white man's diseases of smallpox and cholera that had swept through Indian camps. Buffalo Bill had already gone into show business when General Custer made his famous "last stand" in the Battle of the Little Big Horn in 1876. The famous scout had hurried back to the West, but soon afterward was in show business again.

Buffalo Bill had a kind of show that had never been seen outside of the United States of America. Like the showboat and the minstrel show, it was based on a part of life known only in America. In his show, Buffalo Bill kept alive a little of the old West. He had gathered a company of cowboys and Indians for his actors. He had a small herd of wild buffalo and plenty of western ponies. He gave his show outdoors, without a tent, and his first shows were said to be the "grandfather" of the rodeo as we know it today.

By the time of that New Orleans Fair of the winter of 1884 and 1885, Buffalo Bill's show had many things added to it. He had trick riding and herding of the buffalo, but he also had special acts of western life as it once had been. His actors showed how the stagecoach and Pony Express relays had worked. They staged Indian attacks and battles. Buffalo Bill himself acted out the way he had killed Chief Yellow Hand in revenge for Custer's men.

But Buffalo Bill had run into bad luck as he got ready for the opening in New Orleans. One of his best friends and business partners had died, after a fall from a horse. Then, on the way to New Orleans, the steamboat sank that was carrying his wagons, horses, buffaloes, steers, mules and other show equipment. Most of the animals and wagons were lost.

"Thank goodness the old Deadwood stage coach was saved," Bill said when he learned of it. "It would be impossible to replace it."

Some of his horses had been saved, too, but the buffalo had drowned. He had only half a show ready for New Orleans.

The big fair had a good opening. The exhibits were interesting and people flocked to see them. One of the greatest wonders was the chain of electric lights used on the grounds. But in December a rainy spell began, and few people came to the fair. Most runs of the special trains were without enough passengers to make it worth while to make the trip. They were stopped entirely.

The rains kept on through January. Cowboys and Indians sat around the Buffalo Bill show grounds passing the time as best they could. Over at the Sells Brothers Circus grounds, tents sagged and so did spirits.

Annie and Frank Butler, like all the others in both shows, were in trouble. The shows were not making any money. Actors were going unpaid. The grounds were a sea of mud. Costumes were limp with dampness. Faces were long in all of New Orleans, especially on the grounds of the two shows.

Annie and Frank were sitting in their tent, trying to pass the time. Annie was embroidering a new jacket to wear in her act. Frank picked up a show bill from Buffalo Bill's "Rocky Mountain and Prairie Exhibition."

"Listen to this, Annie," Frank said. He read from the bill. "'Captain A. H. Bogardus, . . . for thirteen years recognized champion of the World and his four marksmen sons . . . .' Annie, you can outshoot Frank

Bogardus and all his sons put together. Let's go over there and see his outfit."

At the race track, there was no sign of a show going on. A sad-faced cowboy directed Annie and Frank to Buffalo Bill's office. The man seated inside had hair hanging to his shoulders and wore a fringed hunting jacket.

"You must be Buffalo Bill," said Frank.

"No, Buffalo Bill is away right now. I'm his manager, Major Burke. Arizona John, they call me."

Frank introduced Annie and himself, and Arizona John's face brightened. He had heard of this little girl — Annie still looked like a little girl, with her brown hair in waves around her shoulders under her broad-brimmed hat.

"I'd like to match my wife against your Captain Bogardus," Frank said. "We might even draw some people to see the match, between rains."

"Bogardus got out of here a week ago and took his boys with him," said Arizona John. "We don't have a crack marksman, outside of Buffalo Bill himself, and young Johnny Baker, who is still learning the tricks."

Annie liked the idea of Buffalo Bill's show, and here was an opening. Before she and Frank left that day, they had arranged to join Buffalo Bill's show in Louisville, Kentucky, in April.

"We're getting a bigger and better show ready for the summer," said Arizona John. "Our bad luck can't last much longer. We'll count on Annie's being in it."

When April came, Frank and Annie went to Louisville. Before they reached the show grounds, they saw a great colored poster on the side of a barn. It showed Buffalo Bill on his big white horse, with a thundering herd of buffalo on the plains behind him. The big red letters gave the show's new name, "BUFFALO BILL'S WILD WEST."

The Wild West company was out on parade when the Butlers reached the great field at the edge of town. Bleachers had been set up for the audience. Across from them were Indian tepees, corrals for the animals and tents for the show people. Annie and Frank were looking around when they heard whoops and war cries and the sound of galloping hoofs. The parade was returning.

"That sounds wonderful. I'll like riding in that kind of parade," Annie said. She and Frank watched the coming of the rattling stagecoach, with the guard pointing his rifle from the high seat, galloping stocky

Indian ponies with riders in full war paint and feathers, weathered cowboys waving their big hats as they rode along, and last of all, still handsome and straight, Buffalo Bill himself on his white horse.

A few minutes later, Buffalo Bill stood before little Annie Oakley, girl of the Ohio backwoods. He swept off his wide-brimmed hat and bowed.

"They told me about you, Missy. We're glad to have you here."

From then on, Annie Oakley was Little Missy. That afternoon and for every Buffalo Bill Wild West Show for the next seventeen years, she opened the show with her act and brought cheers from the crowds who watched.

She dressed in an embroidered jacket and a fringed skirt, with a wide-brimmed hat pushed back on her head. The drums rolled and the trumpets blew a fanfare.

The announcer called out, "Ladies and gentlemen . . . . the foremost woman marksman in the world, in an exhibition of skill with the rifle, shotgun and pistol . . . the little girl of the western plains, Annie Oakley!"

A cowboy on a galloping pony came out first, throwing clay targets into the air. Then came Annie, riding a pony and firing at the targets as she came and never missing a one. Swinging down from the saddle as easily as if she had been riding all her life, she took her place near the gun stand. Frank threw two glass balls into the air. Two bangs of the gun and they were no more. She handled three balls as easily.

Then she turned her back to the flying targets and held up a gleaming knife to use as a mirror. Just as surely, she picked off each target. When she had finished her tricks, each one a little harder than the one before, she swung onto her pony again. Waving her hat at the cheering audience, she rode out of the ring.

She set the tone for the show. People were ready then to see the acting out of war with the Indians, a hold-up of the Deadwood stage, the swift galloping of the Pony Express rider, the herding of buffalo. The American West came to life before their eyes.

Annie, who had never been west of the Mississippi River until she finally traveled there with the show, seemed truly to be the "Girl of the Western Plains," as the poster said. She took the spirit of the West to the great American cities all over the United States, and then to Europe. By that time, the show had a great painted backdrop of Rocky Mountain scenery.

She was the hit of the Wild West Show at the World's Fair in Paris. She played before royalty and before the great people of several nations. To them all, she was the "Girl of the Golden West."

Annie's hair turned white when she was in a train wreck in 1902, but she went on in show business. Her days with the Wild West Show ended soon afterward as the great show closed for the final time. Buffalo Bill died in 1917, last of the great American scouts and star of the greatest of America's pioneering shows. Soon afterward Annie returned to Darke County, Ohio, home again after the full life that began when she sent her quail to the hotels in Cincinnati.

In the hundred years from the time Noah Ludlow and the Drakes took shows westward to the frontier until the end of Buffalo Bill's days, Americans pioneered in show business as in everything else. The whole world had brighter moments because of these "pioneer show folk."